WONDERFUL WORDS

On the Farm!

First published in 2020 by Miles Kelly Publishing Ltd
Harding's Barn, Bardfield End Green, Thaxted, Essex, CM6 3PX, UK

2 4 6 8 10 9 7 5 3 1

Publishing Director Belinda Gallagher
Creative Director Jo Cowan
Senior Editor Amy Johnson
Designer Venita Kidwai
Production Elizabeth Collins, Jenny Brunwin-Jones
Image Manager Liberty Newton
Reprographics Stephan Davis
Assets Lorraine King

ISBN 978-1-78989-117-1

Printed in China

British Library Cataloguing-in-Publication Data
A catalogue record for this book is available from the British Library

Made with paper from a sustainable forest

www.mileskelly.net

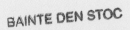
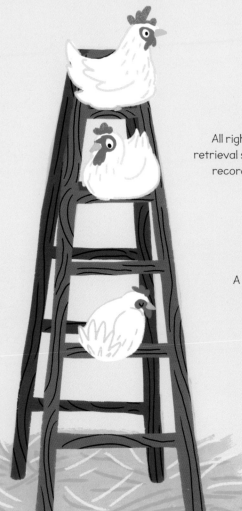

WONDERFUL WORDS

On the Farm!

Illustrated by Louise Pigott

MILES KELLY

At the farm

A farm is a place where food is grown and animals are raised.

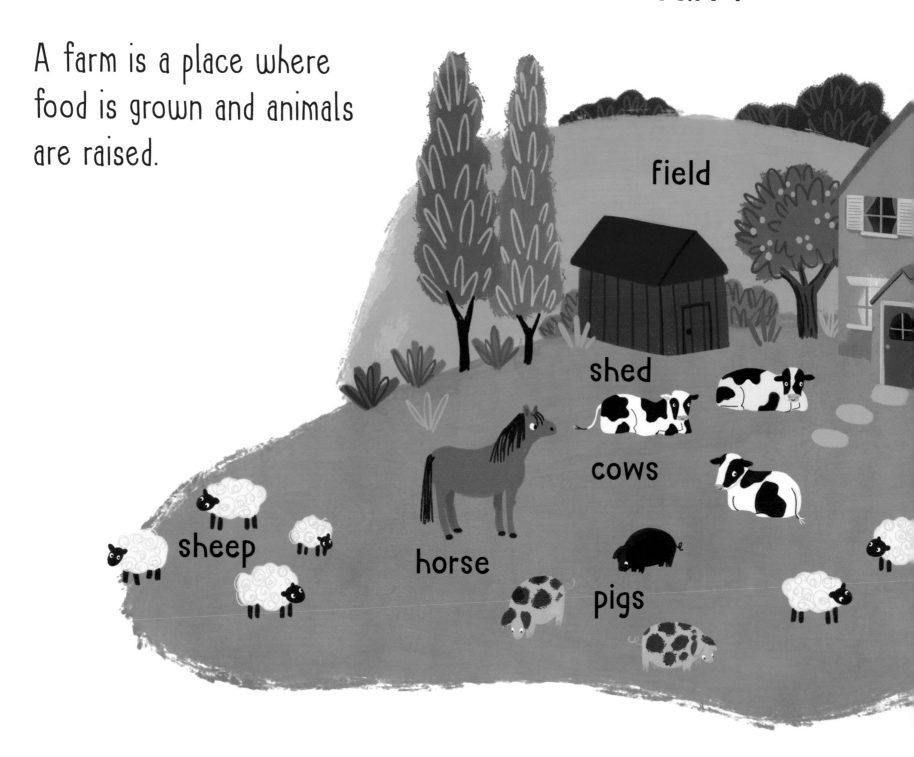

farm

field

shed

cows

horse

pigs

sheep

4

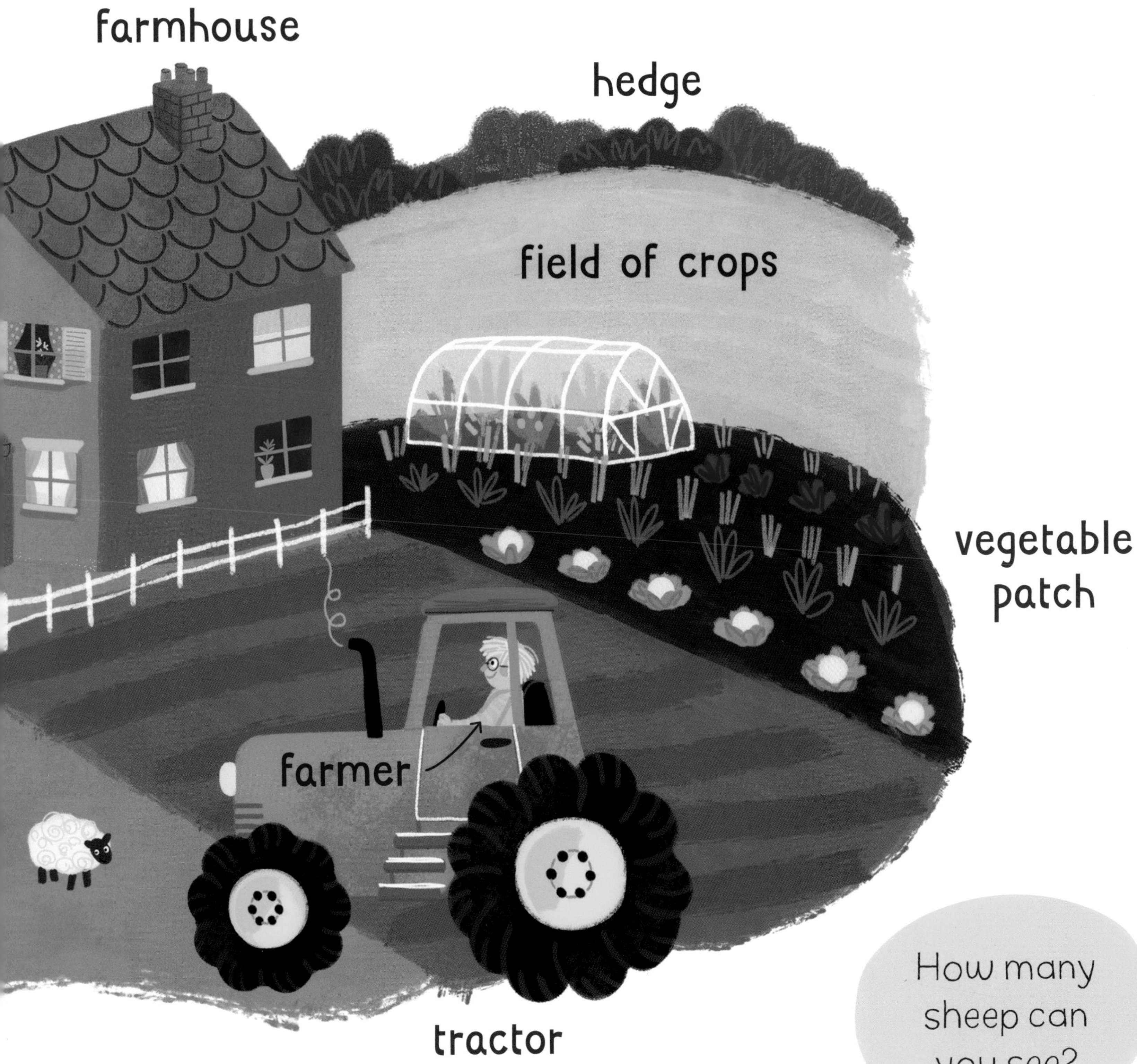

farmhouse

hedge

field of crops

vegetable patch

farmer

tractor

How many sheep can you see?

There are lots of places to store crops and to shelter animals.

silo

barn

hay bales

Grain is stored in a silo.

What colour is the barn?

6

stable

beehive

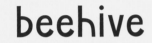

horse

bees

greenhouse

tomatoes

gloves

fork

trowel

What can you see?

You might find all of these useful objects around a farm.

wheelbarrow

spade

rake

Wellies are great for keeping your feet dry!

wellies

What is in the wheelbarrow?

scarecrow

weather vane

bucket

On the move

All sorts of machines help to keep a farm running.

How many hay bales are on the trailer?

tractor

wind turbine

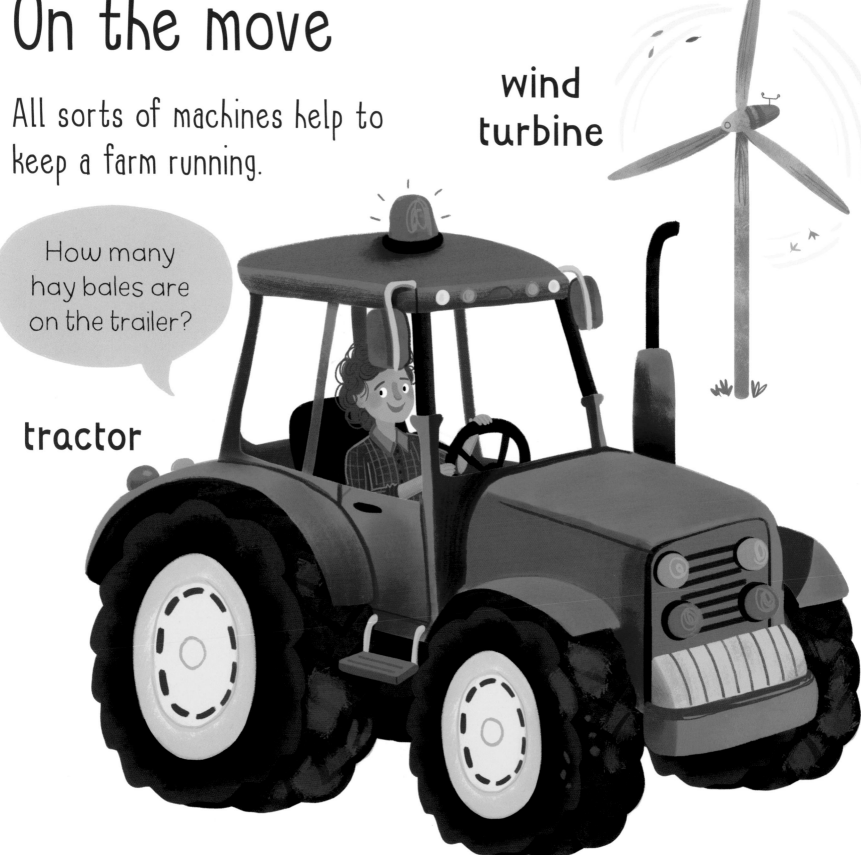

Skid steer loaders are great at digging, and moving straw and mud.

skid steer loader

trailer

pick-up truck

Busy in the fields

Tractors are mainly used to pull other farm machines.

A plough turns the earth, ready for new seeds to be planted.

plough

muck spreader

seed drill

baler

Silage is animal feed made from grass.

silage fork

13

When crops are ripe, harvesters head out to gather them.

The harvester shakes the vine to knock the grapes off.

grape harvester

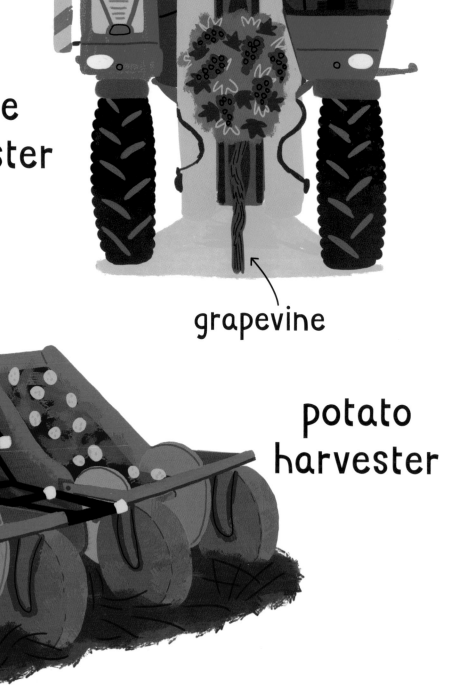

grapevine

potato harvester

potatoes

14

combine harvester

grain

wheat

How many harvesters can you see?

carrots

carrot harvester

Mooooo!

Cows are kept for milk and meat. In some countries, they are also used to pull ploughs.

Hereford cow

Can you find six horns?

16

Highland cattle

horn

cow

calf

We have woolly coats to keep us warm.

buffaloes

Cows are kept in fields and barns.

Friesian cows

Jersey cows

milk tank

How many cows are being milked?

18

bull

hay ring

Charolais
cows

water trough

Fleecy friends

Sheep usually live in groups, called flocks.

Kerry lamb

flock of sheep

Are the ram's horns curly or straight?

ram

hay

sheep pen

sheepdog

Some lambs need to be fed with a bottle.

bottle

shears

sheep shearing

ewe

fleece

lamb

21

Have you ever seen these fleecy farm animals?

What colours can you see on the llama's collar?

alpaca

llama

Angora goat

Lincoln
sheep

Jacob sheep

23

Stuck in the mud

Pigs love to snuffle around and explore.

boar

shelter

Tamworth pig

Saddleback pigs

Count all the curly tails.

sow

piglets

There are many different
kinds of pigs.

spotty pig

What
colour are
my spots?

prize pig

rosette

pig farmer

**Berkshire
piglets**

hairy pig

Are my piglets spotty or stripy?

wild boars

Trotting along

It's fun to ride horses, and to look after them too.

mane

stallion

bridle

tail

reins

Can you spot my four white socks?

saddle

Shetland pony

riding hat

donkey

Donkeys are related to horses.

foal

mare

29

There's always lots going on at the stables.

Shire horse

horsebox

groom

spade

wheelbarrow

dung

bucket

What colour is the horsebox?

rider

pony

jump

farrier

horseshoe

Horseshoes protect a horse's hooves.

Wings and feathers

The farm is busy with clucking chickens.

What colour is the cockerel's tail?

I sit on my eggs to keep them warm.

hen

eggs

nest box

comb

wattles

chicken coop

cockerel

chick

33

Chickens share the farmyard with geese, turkeys and ducks.

turkey

chicken perch

How many goslings can you see?

goose

goslings

feeder

Ducks dabble upside down to eat water plants.

pond

ducks

35

Small animals

Farms often have small animals as well, like these furry friends.

cat

dog

kittens

puppy

Can you find the animal with the biggest ears?

hamster

guinea pig

Do you have a pet?

rabbit

ferret

You might also see some unusual animals!

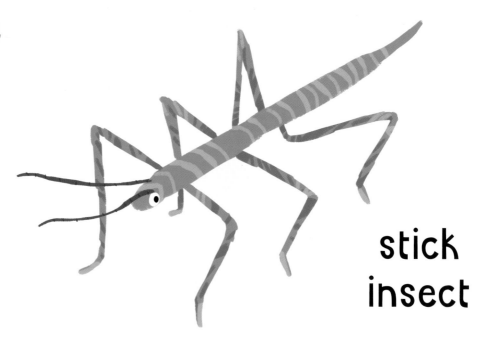

stick insect

peacock

My tail has lots of beautiful eyespots.

tarantula

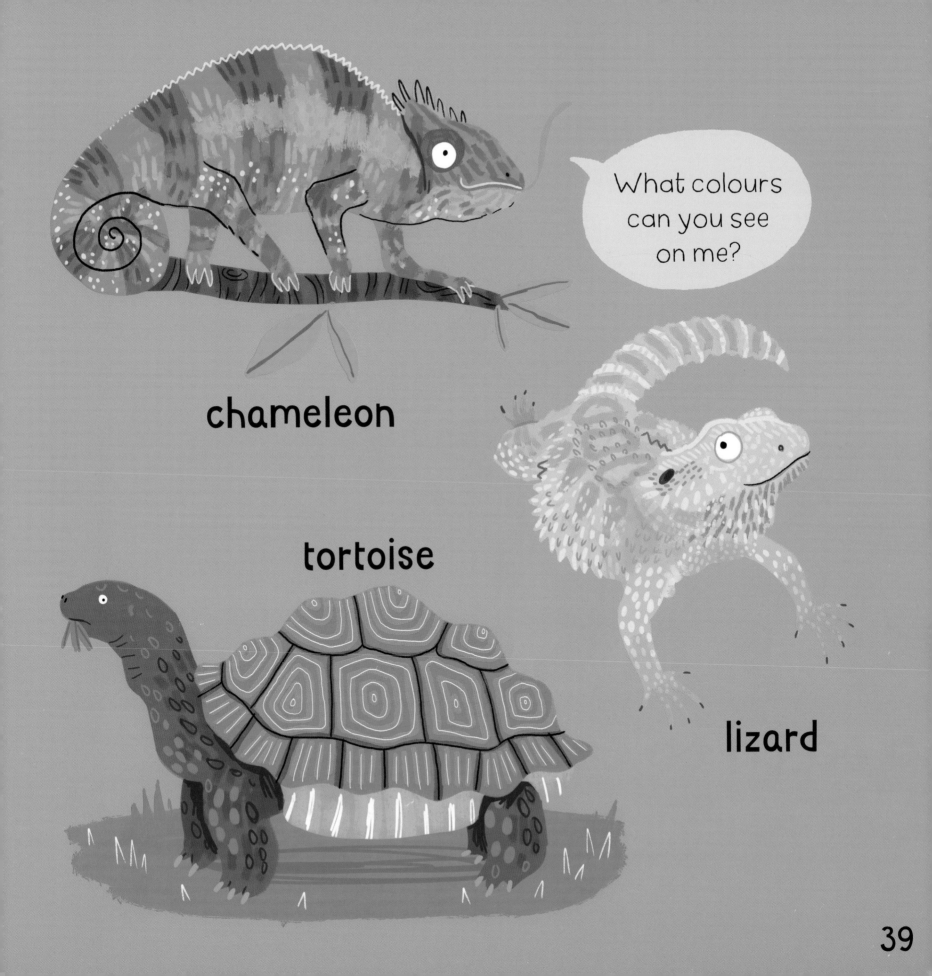

Farm shop

In the shop, you can buy things that are made and grown at the farm.

flour

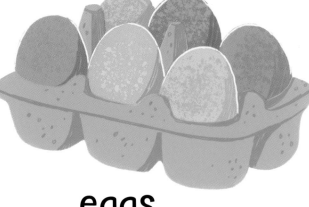

eggs

olives

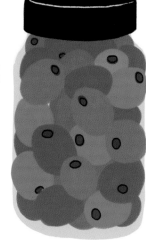

sausage

juice

bread

olive oil

pasta

jam

honey

butter

milk

Can you find two cartons of drink?

cheese

Fruit and vegetables

Different fruit and vegetables are grown in different parts of the world.

strawberries

pear

blueberries

apple tree

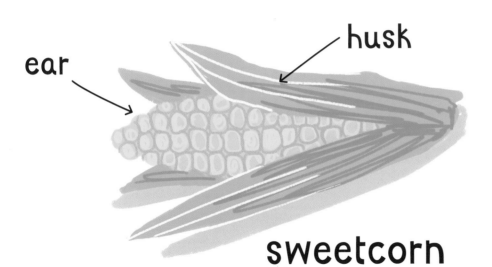

ear

husk

sweetcorn

onion

What colours are the apples?

peppers

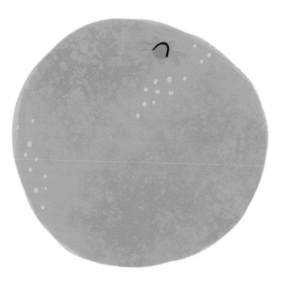

orange

43

Which fruit and vegetables
do you like to eat?

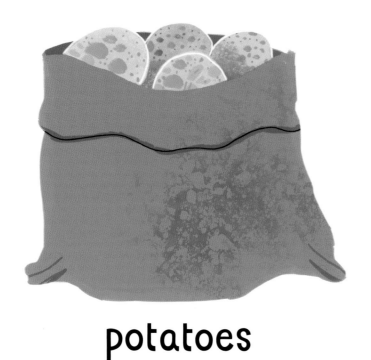

potatoes

broccoli

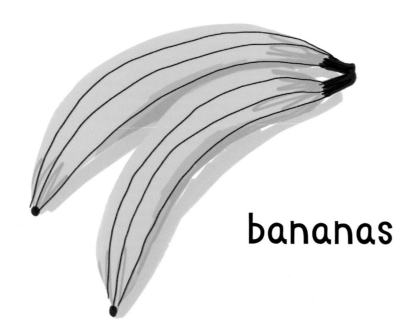

bananas

tomatoes

leeks

grapes

lettuce

Which foods
are green?

carrots

Numbers

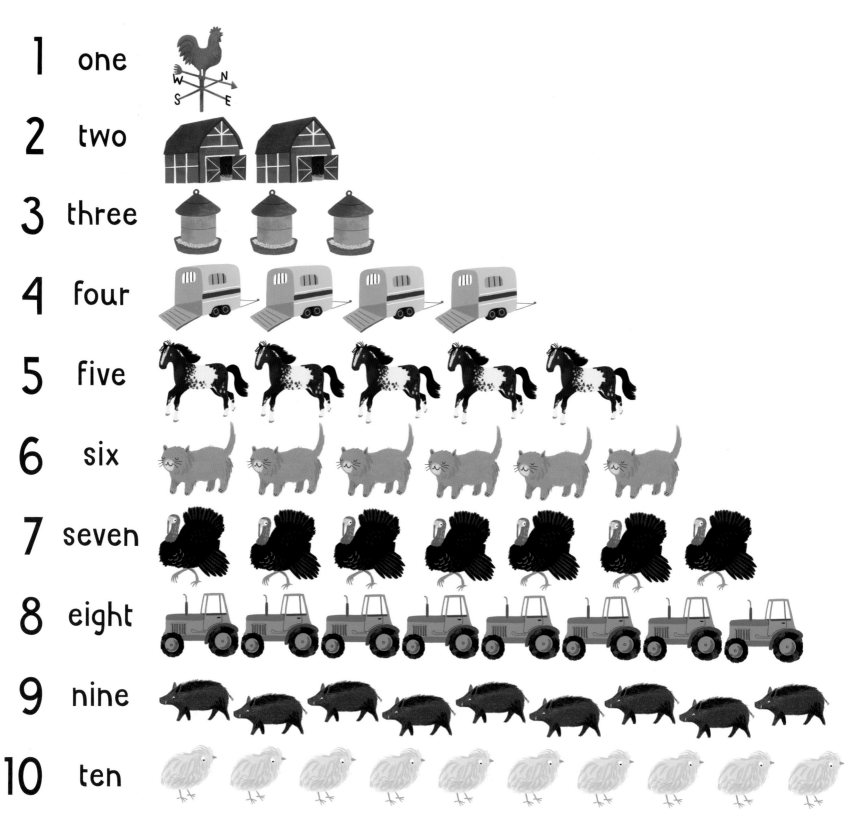

1 one

2 two

3 three

4 four

5 five

6 six

7 seven

8 eight

9 nine

10 ten

11 eleven

12 twelve

13 thirteen

14 fourteen

15 fifteen

16 sixteen

17 seventeen

18 eighteen

19 nineteen

20 twenty

Colours

orange
chicken

pink pig

red
wheelbarrow

blue
farmhouse

grey
donkey

purple
bucket

black
bull

white sheep

brown
cow

yellow
scarecrow

green tractor